The Clouds of Aristophanes

By

Aristophanes

Published by Left of Brain Books

Copyright © 2023 Left of Brain Books

ISBN 978-1-396-32550-2

First Edition

All rights reserved. No part of this publication may be reproduced, distributed, or transmitted in any form or by any means, including photocopying, recording, or other electronic or mechanical methods, without the prior written permission of the publisher, except in the case of brief quotations permitted by copyright law. Left of Brain Books is a division of Left Of Brain Onboarding Pty Ltd.

PUBLISHER'S PREFACE

About the Book

"The Clouds (Nephelae) is a comedy written by the Ancient Greek playwright Aristophanes lampooning the sophists and the intellectual trends of late fifth-century Athens. Although it took last place in the comic festival Aristophanes entered it in, it is one of his most famous works because it offers a highly unusual portrayal of Socrates. Many also find the play to be quite funny as an irreverent satire of pretentious academia.

Aristophanes re-wrote the play after its initial failure, inserting an interlude into the middle of the action in which the playwright himself takes the stage and chastizes the audience for their poor sense of humor. Thus the play can also be regarded as one of the first instances of self-referential or post-modern literature.

The play opens with a citizen of Athens, Strepsiades (whose name, loosely translated, means slippery, deceptive, twisty, or scheming), bemoaning the addiction of Pheidippides, his pretty-boy son, to horse-racing, and buying of expensive items and horses which has put him into deep debt. He recalls his own humble upbringing on a farm and curses his marriage to an aristocratic city woman, whose wealth he believes is responsible for spoiling his son. Pheidippides refuses to get a job. Socrates emerges in the play, explaining his descent from the heavens, and enters into dialog with Strepsiades."

(Quote from wikipedia.org)

About the Author

"Aristophanes, son of Philippus, was a Greek Old Comic dramatist. He is also known as the Father of Comedy and the Prince of Ancient Comedy.

The place and exact date of his birth are unknown, but he was around thirty in the 420s BC when he achieved sudden brilliant success in the Theater of Dionysus with his Banqueters. He lived in the deme of Kudathenaion (the same as that of the leading Athenian statesman Cleon) which implies he was from a relatively wealthy family and, accordingly, well educated. He is famous for writing comedies such as The Birds for the two Athenian dramatic festivals: the City Dionysia and the Lenaia. He wrote forty plays, eleven of which survive; his plays are the only surviving complete examples of Old Attic Comedy, although extensive fragments of the work of his rough contemporaries Cratinus and Eupolis survive. Many of Aristophanes' plays were political, and often satirized well-known citizens of Athens and their conduct in the Peloponnesian War and after. Hints in the text of his plays, supported by ancient scholars, suggest that he was prosecuted several times by Cleon for defaming Athens in the presence of foreigners and the like; how much truth there is to this is impossible to say. The Frogs was given the unprecedented honor of a second performance. According to a later biographer, he was also awarded a civic crown for the play."

(Quote from wikipedia.org)

CONTENTS

PUBLISHER'S PREFACE
DRAMATIS PERSONAE 1
   THE CLOUDS OF ARISTOPHANES 2

DRAMATIS PERSONAE

Strepsiades
Phidippides
Servant of Strepsiades
Disciples of Socrates
Socrates
Chorus of Clouds
Just Cause
Unjust Cause
Pasias
Amynias
Witness
Chaerephon

THE CLOUDS OF ARISTOPHANES

Scene: The interior of a sleeping-apartment: Strepsiades, Phidippides, and two servants are in their beds; a small house is seen at a distance. Time: midnight.

Strepsiades
(sitting up in his bed).
Ah me! Ah me! O King Jupiter, of what a terrible length the nights are! Will it never be day? And yet long since I heard the cock. My domestics are snoring; but they would not have one so heretofore! May you perish then, O war! For many reasons; because I may not even punish my domestics. Neither does this excellent youth awake through the night; but takes his ease, wrapped up in five blankets. Well, if it is the fashion, let us snore wrapped up.

[Lies down, and then almost immediately starts up again.]

But I am not able, miserable man, to sleep, being tormented by my expenses, and my stud of horses, and my ebts, through this son of mine. He with his long hair, is riding horses and driving curricles, and dreaming of orses; while I am driven to distraction, as I see the moon bringing on the twentieths; for the interest is running on. Boy! Light a lamp, and bring forth my tablets, that I may take them and read to how many I am indebted, and calculate the interest.

[Enter boy with a light and tablets.]

Come, let me see; what do I owe? Twelve minae to Pasias.

Why twelve minae to Pasias? Why did I borrow them? When I bought the blood-horse. Ah me, unhappy!
Would that it had had its eye knocked out with a stone first!

Phidippides

(talking in his sleep).

You are acting unfairly, Philo! Drive on your own course.

Strep.

This is the bane that has destroyed me; for even in his sleep he dreams about horsemanship.

Phid.

How many courses will the war-chariots run?

Strep.

Many courses do you drive me, your father. But what debt came upon me after Pasias? Three minae to Amynias for a little chariot and pair of wheels.

Phid.

Lead the horse home, after having given him a good rolling.

Strep.

O foolish youth, you have rolled me out of my possessions; since I have been cast in suits, and others say that they will have surety given them for the
interest.

Phid.

(awakening) Pray, father, why are you peevish, and toss about the whole night?

Strep.

A bailiff out of the bedclothes is biting me.

Phid.

Suffer me, good sir, to sleep a little.

Strep.

Then, do you sleep on; but know that all these debts will turn on your head.

[Phidippides falls asleep again.]

Alas! Would that the match-maker had perished miserably, who induced me to marry your mother. For a country life used to be most agreeable to me, dirty, untrimmed, reclining at random, abounding in bees, and sheep, and oil-cake. Then I, a rustic, married a niece of Megacles, the son of Megacles, from the city, haughty, luxurious, and Coesyrafied. When I married her, I lay with her redolent of new wine, of the cheese-crate, and abundance of wool; but she, on the contrary, of ointment, saffron, wanton-kisses, extravagance, gluttony, and of Colias and Genetyllis. I will not indeed say that she was idle; but she wove. And I used to show her this cloak by way of a pretext and say "Wife, you weave at a great rate."

[Servant re-enters.]

Servant.
We have no oil in the lamp.
Strep.
Ah me! Why did you light the thirsty lamp? Come hither that you may weep!
Ser.
For what, pray, shall I weep?
Strep.
Because you put in one of the thick wicks.

[Servant runs out]

After this, when this son was born to us, to me, orsooth, and to my excellent wife, we squabbled then about the name: for she was for adding hippos to the name, Xanthippus, or Charippus, or Callipides; but I was or giving him the name of his grandfather, Phidonides.
For a time therefore we disputed; and then at length we agreed, and called him Phidippides. She used to take this

son and fondle him, saying, "When you, being grown up, shall drive your chariot to the city, like Megacles, with a xystis." But I used to say, "Nay, rather, when dressed in a leathern jerkin, you shall drive goats from Phelleus, like your father." He paid no attention to my words, but poured a horse-fever over my property. Now, therefore, by meditating the whole night, I have discovered one path for my course extraordinarily excellent; to which if I persuade this youth I shall be saved. But first I wish to awake him. How then can I awake him in the most agreeable manner? How? Phidippides, my little Phidippides?

Phid.

What, father?

Strep.

Kiss me, and give me your right hand!

Phid.

There. What's the matter?

Strep.

Tell me, do you love me?

Phid.

Yes, by this Equestrian Neptune.

Strep.

Nay, do not by any means mention this Equestrian to me, for this god is the author of my misfortunes.

But, if you really love me from your heart, my son, obey me.

Phid.

In what then, pray, shall I obey you?

Strep.

Reform your habits as quickly as possible, and go and learn what I advise.

Phid.

Tell me now, what do you prescribe?

Strep.

And will you obey me at all?

Phid.

By Bacchus, I will obey you.

Strep.

Look this way then! Do you see this little door and little house?

Phid.

I see it. What then, pray, is this, father?

Strep.

This is a thinking-shop of wise spirits. There dwell men who in speaking of the heavens persuade people that it is an oven, and that it encompasses us, and that we are the embers. These men teach, if one give them money, to conquer in speaking, right or wrong.

Phid.

Who are they?

Strep.

I do not know the name accurately. They are minute philosophers, noble and excellent.

Phid.

Bah! They are rogues; I know them. You mean the quacks, the pale-faced wretches, the bare-footed fellows, of whose numbers are the miserable Socrates and Chaerephon.

Strep.

Hold! Hold! Be silent! Do not say anything foolish. But, if you have any concern for your father's patrimony, become one of them, having given up your horsemanship.

Phid.

I would not, by Bacchus, even if you were to give me the pheasants which Leogoras rears!

Strep.

Go, I entreat you, dearest of men, go and be taught.

Phid.

Why, what shall I learn?

Strep.

They say that among them are both the two causes--the better cause, whichever that is, and the worse: they say that the one of these two causes, the worse, prevails, though it speaks on the unjust side.

If, therefore you learn for me this unjust cause, I would not pay any one, not even an obolus of these debts, which I owe at present on your account.

Phid.

I can not comply; for I should not dare to look upon the knights, having lost all my colour.

Strep.

Then, by Ceres, you shall not eat any of my good! Neither you, nor your blood-horse; but I will drive you out of my house to the crows.

Phid.

My uncle Megacles will not permit me to be without a horse. But I'll go in, and pay no heed to you.

[Exit Phidippides.]

Strep.

Though fallen, still I will not lie prostrate: but having prayed to the gods, I will go myself to the thinking-shop and get taught. How, then, being an old man, shall I learn the subtleties of refined disquisitions? I must go. Why thus do I loiter and not knock at the door?

[Knocks at the door.]

Boy! Little boy!

Disciple (from within). Go to the devil! Who it is that knocked at the door?

Strep.

Strepsiades, the son of Phidon, of Cicynna.

Dis.
> You are a stupid fellow, by Jove! who have kicked against the door so very carelessly, and have caused the miscarriage of an idea which I had conceived.

Strep.
> Pardon me; for I dwell afar in the country. But tell me the thing which has been made to miscarry.

Dis.
> It is not lawful to mention it, except to disciples.

Strep.
> Tell it, then, to me without fear; for I here am come as a disciple to the thinking-shop.

Dis.
> I will tell you; but you must regard these as mysteries. Socrates lately asked Chaerephon about a flea, how many of its own feet it jumped; for after having bit the eyebrow of Chaerephon, it leaped away onto the head of Socrates.

Strep.
> How then did he measure this?

Dis.
> Most cleverly. He melted some wax; and then took the flea and dipped its feet in the wax; and then a pair of Persian slippers stuck to it when cooled. Having gently loosened these, he measured back the distance.

Strep.
> O King Jupiter! What subtlety of thought!

Dis.
> What then would you say if you heard another contrivance of Socrates?

Strep.
> Of what kind? Tell me, I beseech you!

Dis.
> Chaerephon the Sphettian asked him whether he thought gnats buzzed through the mouth or the breech.

Strep.

What, then, did he say about the gnat?
Dis.
He said the intestine of the gnat was narrow and that the wind went forcibly through it, being slender, straight to the breech; and then that the rump, being hollow where it is adjacent to the narrow part, resounded through the violence of the wind.
Strep.
The rump of the gnats then is a trumpet! Oh, thrice happy he for his sharp-sightedness! Surely a defendant might easily get acquitted who understands the intestine of the gnat.
Dis.
But he was lately deprived of a great idea by a lizard.
Strep.
In what way? Tell me.
Dis.
As he was investigating the courses of the moon and her revolutions, then as he was gaping upward a lizard in the darkness dropped upon him from the roof.
Strep.
I am amused at a lizard's having dropped on Socrates.
Dis.
Yesterday evening there was no supper for us.
Strep.
Well. What then did he contrive for provisions?
Dis.
He sprinkled fine ashes on the table, and bent a little spit, and then took it as a pair of compasses and filched a cloak from the Palaestra.
Strep.
Why then do we admire Thales? Open open quickly the thinking-shop, and show to me Socrates as quickly as possible. For I desire to be a disciple. Come, open the

door.

[The door of the thinking-shop opens and the pupils of Socrates are seen all with their heads fixed on the ground, while Socrates himself is seen suspended in the air in a basket.]

O Hercules, from what country are these wild beasts?

Dis.

What do you wonder at? To what do they seem to you to be like?

Strep.

To the Spartans who were taken at Pylos. But why in the world do these look upon the ground?

Dis.

They are in search of the things below the earth.

Strep.

Then they are searching for roots. Do not, then, trouble yourselves about this; for I know where there are large and fine ones. Why, what are these doing, who are bent down so much?

Dis.

These are groping about in darkness under Tartarus.

Strep.

Why then does their rump look toward heaven?

Dis.

It is getting taught astronomy alone by itself.

[Turning to the pupils.]

But go in, lest he meet with us.

Strep.

Not yet, not yet; but let them remain, that I may communicate to them a little matter of my own.

Dis.

It is not permitted to them to remain without in the open air for a very long time.

[The pupils retire.]

Strep.
(discovering a variety of mathematical instruments) Why, what is this, in the name of heaven?
Tell me.
Dis.
This is Astronomy.
Strep.
But what is this?
Dis.
Geometry.
Strep.
What then is the use of this?
Dis.
To measure out the land.
Strep.
What belongs to an allotment?
Dis.
No, but the whole earth.
Strep.
You tell me a clever notion; for the contrivance is democratic and useful.
Dis.
(pointing to a map) See, here's a map of the whole earth. Do you see? This is Athens.
Strep.
What say you? I don't believe you; for I do not see the Dicasts sitting.
Dis.
Be assured that this is truly the Attic territory.
Strep.
Why, where are my fellow-tribesmen of Cicynna?

Dis.
>Here they are. And Euboea here, as you see, is stretched out a long way by the side of it to a great distance.

Strep.
>I know that; for it was stretched by us and Pericles. But where is Lacedaemon?

Dis.
>Where is it? Here it is.

Strep.
>How near it is to us! Pay great attention to this, to remove it very far from us.

Dis.
>By Jupiter, it is not possible.

Strep.
>Then you will weep for it.

[Looking up and discovering Socrates.]

>Come, who is this man who is in the basket?

Dis.
>Himself.

Strep.
>Who's "Himself"?

Dis.
>Socrates.

Strep.
>O Socrates! Come, you sir, call upon him loudly for me.

Dis.
>Nay, rather, call him yourself; for I have no leisure.

[Exit Disciple.]

Strep.
>Socrates! My little Socrates!

Socrates.

Why callest thou me, thou creature of a day?
Strep.
First tell me, I beseech you, what are you doing.
Soc.
I am walking in the air, and speculating about the sun.
Strep.
And so you look down upon the gods from your basket, and not from the earth?
Soc.
For I should not have rightly discovered things celestial if I had not suspended the intellect, and mixed the thought in a subtle form with its kindred air.

But if, being on the ground, I speculated from below on things above, I should never have discovered them. For the earth forcibly attracts to itself the meditative moisture. Water-cresses also suffer the very same thing.
Strep.
What do you say? Does meditation attract the moisture to the water-cresses? Come then, my little
Socrates, descend to me, that you may teach me those things, for the sake of which I have come.

[Socrates lowers himself and gets out of the basket.]

Soc.
And for what did you come?
Strep.
Wishing to learn to speak; for by reason of usury, and most ill-natured creditors, I am pillaged and plundered, and have my goods seized for debt.
Soc.
How did you get in debt without observing it?
Strep.
A horse-disease consumed me--terrible at eating.

But teach me the other one of your two causes, that which pays nothing; and I will swear by the gods, I will pay down to you whatever reward you exact of me.

Soc.

By what gods will you swear? For, in the first place, gods are not a current coin with us.

Strep.

By what do you swear? By iron money, as in Byzantium?

Soc.

Do you wish to know clearly celestial matters, what they rightly are?

Strep.

Yes, by Jupiter, if it be possible!

Soc.

And to hold converse with the Clouds, our divinities?

Strep.

By all means.

Soc.

(with great solemnity). Seat yourself, then, upon the sacred couch.

Strep.

Well, I am seated!

Soc.

Take, then, this chaplet.

Strep.

For what purpose a chaplet? Ah me! Socrates, see that you do not sacrifice me like Athamas!

Strep.

No; we do all these to those who get initiated.

Strep.

Then what shall I gain, pray?

Soc.

You shall become in oratory a tricky knave, a thorough rattle, a subtle speaker. But keep quiet.

Strep.

By Jupiter! You will not deceive me; for if I am besprinkled, I shall become fine flour.

Soc.
It becomes the old man to speak words of good omen, and to hearken to my prayer. O sovereign King, immeasurable Air, who keepest the earth suspended, and through bright Aether, and ye august goddesses, the Clouds, sending thunder and lightning, arise, appear in the air, O mistresses, to your deep thinker!

Strep.
Not yet, not yet, till I wrap this around me lest I be wet through. To think of my having come from home without even a cap, unlucky man!

Soc.
Come then, ye highly honoured Clouds, for a display to this man. Whether ye are sitting upon the sacred snow-covered summits of Olympus, or in the gardens of Father Ocean form a sacred dance with the Nymphs, or draw in golden pitchers the streams of the waters of the Nile, or inhabit the Maeotic lake, or the snowy rock of Mimas, hearken to our prayer, and receive the sacrifice, and be propitious to the sacred rites.

[The following song is heard at a distance, accompanied by loud claps of thunder.]

Chorus.
Eternal Clouds! Let us arise to view with our dewy, clear-bright nature, from loud-sounding Father Ocean to the wood-crowned summits of the lofty mountains, in order that we may behold clearly the far-seen watch-towers, and the fruits, and the fostering, sacred earth, and the rushing sounds of the divine rivers, and the roaring, loud-sounding sea; for the unwearied eye of Aether sparkles with glittering

rays. Come, let us shake off the watery cloud from our immortal forms and survey the earth with far-seeing eye.

Soc.
O ye greatly venerable Clouds, ye have clearly heard me when I called.

[Turning to Strepsiades.]

Did you hear the voice, and the thunder which bellowed at the same time, feared as a god?

Strep.
I too worship you, O ye highly honoured, and am inclined to reply to the thundering, so much do I tremble at them and am alarmed. And whether it be lawful, or be not lawful, I have a desire just now to ease myself.

Soc.
Don't scoff, nor do what these poor-devil-poets do, but use words of good omen, for a great swarm of goddesses is in motion with their songs.

Cho.
Ye rain-bringing virgins, let us come to the fruitful land of Pallas, to view the much-loved country of Cecrops, abounding in brave men; where is reverence for sacred rites not to be divulged; where the house that receives the initiated is thrown open in holy mystic rites; and gifts to the celestial gods; and high-roofed temples, and statues; and most sacred processions in honour of the blessed gods; and well-crowned sacrifices to the gods, and feasts, at all seasons; and with the approach of spring the Bacchic festivity, and the rousings of melodious choruses, and the loud-sounding music of flutes.

Strep.
Tell me, O Socrates, I beseech you, by Jupiter, who are these that have uttered this grand song? Are they some heroines?

Soc.
> By no means; but heavenly Clouds, great divinities to idle men; who supply us with thought and argument, and intelligence and humbug, and circumlocution, and ability to hoax, and comprehension.

Strep.
> On this account therefore my soul, having heard their voice, flutters, and already seeks to discourse subtilely, and to quibble about smoke, and having pricked a maxim with a little notion, to refute the opposite argument. So that now I eagerly desire, if by any means it be possible, to see them palpably.

Soc.
> Look, then, hither, toward Mount Parnes; for now I behold them descending gently.

Strep.
> Pray where? Show me.

Soc.
> See! There they come in great numbers through the hollows and thickets; there, obliquely.

Strep.
> What's the matter? For I can't see them.

Soc.
> By the entrance.

[Enter Chorus]

Strep.
> Now at length with difficulty I just see them.

Soc.
> Now at length you assuredly see them, unless you have your eyes running pumpkins.

Strep.

Yes, by Jupiter! O highly honoured Clouds, for now they cover all things.

Soc.

Did you not, however, know, nor yet consider, these to be goddesses?

Strep.

No, by Jupiter! But I thought them to be mist, and dew, and smoke.

Soc.

For you do not know, by Jupiter! that these feed very many sophists, Thurian soothsayers, practisers of medicine, lazy-long-haired-onyx-ring-wearers, song-twisters for the cyclic dances, and meteorological quacks. They feed idle people who do nothing, because such men celebrate them in verse.

Strep.

For this reason, then, they introduced into their erses "the dreadful impetuosity of the moist, whirling-bright clouds"; and the "curls of hundred-headed Typho"; and the "hard-blowing tempests"; and then "aerial, moist"; "crooked-clawed birds, floating in air"' and "the showers of rain from dewy Clouds." And then, in return for these, they swallow "slices of great, fine mullets, and bird's-flesh of thrushes."

Soc.

Is it not just, however, that they should have their reward, on account of these?

Strep.

Tell me, pray, if they are really clouds, what ails them, that they resemble mortal women? For they are not such.

Soc.

Pray, of what nature are they?

Strep.

I do not clearly know: at any rate they resemble spread-out fleeces, and not women, by Jupiter! Not a bit; for these have noses.

Soc.

Answer, then, whatever I ask you.
Strep.
Then say quickly what you wish.
Soc.
Have you ever, when you; looked up, seen a cloud like to a centaur, or a panther, or a wolf, or a bull?
Strep.
By Jupiter, have I! But what of that?
Soc.
They become all things, whatever they please. And then if they see a person with long hair, a wild one of these hairy fellows, like the son of Xenophantes, in derision of his folly, they liken themselves to centaurs.
Strep.
Why, what, if they should see Simon, a plunderer of the public property, what do they do?
Soc.
They suddenly become wolves, showing up his disposition.
Strep.
For this reason, then, for this reason, when they yesterday saw Cleonymus the recreant, on this account they became stags, because they saw this most cowardly fellow.
Soc.
And now too, because they saw Clisthenes, you observe, on this account they became women.
Strep.
Hail therefore, O mistresses! And now, if ever ye did to any other, to me also utter a voice reaching to heaven, O all-powerful queens.
Cho.
Hail, O ancient veteran, hunter after learned speeches! And thou, O priest of most subtle trifles!
Tell us what you require? For we would not hearken to any other of the recent meteorological sophists, except to Pro-

dicus; to him, on account of his wisdom and intelligence; and to you, because you walk proudly in the streets, and cast your eyes askance, and endure many hardships with bare feet, and in reliance upon us lookest supercilious.

Strep.

O Earth, what a voice! How holy and dignified and wondrous!

Soc.

For, in fact, these alone are goddesses; and all the rest is nonsense.

Strep.

But come, by the Earth, is not Jupiter, the Olympian, a god?

Soc.

What Jupiter? Do not trifle. There is no Jupiter.

Strep.

What do you say? Who rains then? For first of all explain this to me.

Soc.

These to be sure. I will teach you it by powerful evidence. Come, where have you ever seen him raining at any time without Clouds? And yet he ought to rain in fine weather, and these be absent.

Strep.

By Apollo, of a truth you have rightly confirmed this by your present argument. And yet, before this, I really thought that Jupiter caused the rain. But tell me who is it that thunders. This makes me tremble.

Soc.

These, as they roll, thunder.

Strep.

In what way? you all-daring man!

Soc.

When they are full of much water, and are compelled to be borne along, being necessarily precipitated when full of rain, then they fall heavily upon each other and burst and clap.

Strep.
Who is it that compels them to borne along? Is it not Jupiter?

Soc.
By no means, but aethereal Vortex.

Strep.
Vortex? It had escaped my notice that Jupiter did not exist, and that Vortex now reigned in his stead. But you have taught me nothing as yet concerning the clap and the thunder.

Soc.
Have you not heard me, that I said that the Clouds, when full of moisture, dash against each other and clap by reason of their density?

Strep.
Come, how am I to believe this?

Soc.
I'll teach you from your own case. Were you ever, after being stuffed with broth at the Panathenaic festival, then disturbed in your belly, and did a tumult suddenly rumble through it?

Strep.
Yes, by Apollo! And immediately the little broth plays the mischief with me, and is disturbed and rumbles like thunder, and grumbles dreadfully: at first gently pappax, pappax; and then it adds papa-pappax; and finally, it thunders downright papapappax, as they do.

Soc.
Consider, therefore, how you have trumpeted from a little belly so small; and how is it not probable that this air, being boundless, should thunder so loudly?

Strep.

For this reason, therefore, the two names also Trump and Thunder, are similar to each other. But teach me this, whence comes the thunderbolt blazing with fire, and burns us to ashes when it smites us, and singes those who survive. For indeed Jupiter evidently hurls this at the perjured.

Soc.
Why, how then, you foolish person, and savouring of the dark ages and antediluvian, if his manner is to smite the perjured, does he not blast Simon, and Cleonymus, and Theorus? And yet they are very perjured. But he smites his own temple, and Sunium the promontory of Athens, and the tall oaks. Wherefore, for indeed an oak does not commit perjury.

Strep.
I do not know; but you seem to speak well. For what, pray, is the thunderbolt?

Soc.
When a dry wind, having been raised aloft, is inclosed in these Clouds, it inflates them within, like a bladder; and then, of necessity, having burst them, it rushes out with vehemence by reason of its density, setting fire to itself through its rushing and impetuosity.

Strep.
By Jupiter, of a truth I once experienced this exactly at the Diasian festival! I was roasting a haggis for my kinsfolk, and through neglect I did not cut it open; but it became inflated and then suddenly bursting, befouled my eyes and burned my face.

Cho.
O mortal, who hast desired great wisdom from us!
How happy will you become among the Athenians and among the Greeks, if you be possessed of a good memory, and be a deep thinker, and endurance of labour be implanted in your soul, and you be not wearied either by standing or walking, nor be exceedingly vexed at shivering

with cold, nor long to break your fast, and you refrain from wine, and gymnastics, and the other follies, and consider this the highest excellence, as is proper a clever man should, to conquer by action and counsel, and by battling with your tongue.

Strep.
As far as regards a sturdy spirit, and care that makes one's bed uneasy, and a frugal spirit and hard-living and savory-eating belly, be of good courage and don't trouble yourself; I would offer myself to hammer on, for that matter.

Soc.
Will you not, pray, now believe in no god, except what we believe in--this Chaos, and the Clouds, and the Tongue--these three?

Strep.
Absolutely I would not even converse with the others, not even if I met them; nor would I sacrifice to them, nor make libations, nor offer frankincense.

Cho.
Tell us then boldly, what we must do for you? For you shall not fail in getting it, if you honour and admire us, and seek to become clever.

Strep.
O mistresses, I request of you then this very small favour, that I be the best of the Greeks in speaking by a hundred stadia.

Cho.
Well, you shall have this from us, so that hence-forward from this time no one shall get more opinions passed in the public assemblies than you.

Strep.
Grant me not to deliver important opinions; for I do not desire these, but only to pervert the right for my own advantage, and to evade my creditors.

Cho.
> Then you shall obtain what you desire; for you do not covet great things. But commit yourself without fear to our ministers.

Strep.
> I will do so in reliance upon you, for necessity oppresses me, on account of the blood-horses, and the marriage that ruined me. Now, therefore, let them use me as they please. I give up this body to them to be beaten, to be hungered, to be troubled with thirst, to be squalid, to shiver with cold, to flay into a leathern bottle, if I shall escape clear from my debts, and appear to men to be bold, glib of tongue, audacious, impudent, shameless, a fabricator of falsehoods, inventive of words, a practiced knave in lawsuits, a law-tablet, a thorough rattle, a fox, a sharper, a slippery knave, a dissembler, a slippery fellow, an impostor, a gallows-bird, a blackguard, a twister, a troublesome fellow, a licker-up of hashes. If they call me this, when they meet me, let them do to me absolutely what they please. And if they like, by Ceres, let them serve up a sausage out of me to the deep thinkers.

Cho.
> This man has a spirit not void of courage, but prompt. Know, that if you learn these matters from me, you will possess among mortals a glory as high as
> heaven.

Strep.
> What shall I experience?

Cho.
> You shall pass with me the most enviable of mortal lives the whole time.

Strep.
> Shall I then ever see this?

Cho.

Yea, so that many be always seated at your gates, wishing to communicate with you and come to a conference with you, to consult with you as to actions and affidavits of many talents, as is worthy of your abilities.

[To Socrates.]

But attempt to teach the old man by degrees whatever you urpose, and scrutinize his intellect, and make trial of his mind.
Soc.
Come now, tell me your own turn of mind; in order that, when I know of what sort it is, I may now, after this, apply to you new engines.
Strep.
What? By the gods, do you purpose to besiege me?
Soc.
No; I wish to briefly learn from you if you are possessed of a good memory.
Strep.
In two ways, by Jove! If anything be owing to me, I have a very good memory; but if I owe unhappy man, I am very forgetful.
Soc.
Is the power of speaking, pray, implanted in your nature?
Strep.
Speaking is not in me, but cheating is.
Soc.
How, then, will you be able to learn?
Strep.
1Excellently, of course.
Soc.

Come, then, take care that, whenever I propound any clever dogma about abstruse matters, you catch it up immediately.

Strep.

What then? Am I to feed upon wisdom like a dog?

Soc.

This man is ignorant and brutish--I fear, old man, lest you will need blows. Come, let me see; what do you do if any one beat you?

Strep.

I take the beating; and then, when I have waited a little while, I call witnesses to prove it; then again, after a short interval, I go to law.

Soc.

Come, then, lay down your cloak.

Strep.

Have I done any wrong?

Soc.

No; but it is the rule to enter naked.

Strep.

But I do not enter to search for stolen goods.

Soc.

Lay it down. Why do you talk nonsense?

Strep.

Now tell me this, pray. If I be diligent and learn zealously, to which of your disciples shall I become like?

Soc.

You will no way differ from Chaerephon in intellect.

Strep.

Ah me, unhappy! I shall become half-dead.

Soc.

Don't chatter; but quickly follow me hither with smartness.

Strep.

Then give me first into my hands a honeyed cake; for I am afraid of descending within, as if into the cave of Trophonius.

Soc.
Proceed; why do you keep poking about the door?

[Exeunt Socrates and Strepsiades]

Cho.
Well, go in peace, for the sake of this your valour. May prosperity attend the man, because, being advanced into the vale of years, he imbues his intellect with modern subjects, and cultivates wisdom!

[Turning to the audience.]

Spectators, I will freely declare to you the truth, by Bacchus, who nurtured me! So may I conquer, and be accounted skillful, as that, deeming you to be clever spectators, and this to be the cleverest of my comedies, I thought proper to let you first taste that comedy, which gave me the greatest labour. And then I retired from the contest defeated by vulgar fellows, though I did not deserve it. These things, therefore, I object to you, a learned audience, for whose sake I was expending this labour. But not even thus will I ever willingly desert the discerning portion of you. For since what time my Modest Man and my Rake were very highly praised here by an audience, with whom it is a pleasure even to hold converse, and I (for I was still a virgin, and it was not lawful for me as yet to have children) exposed my offspring, and another girl took it up, and owned it, and you generously reared and educated it, from this time I have had sure pledges of your good will toward me. Now, therefore, like that well-known Electra, has this comedy come seeking, if haply it meet with an audience so clever, for it will recognize, if it should see, the lock of its brother. But see how modest she is by nature, who, in the first place, has come, having stitched to her no leathern phallus hanging down, red at the top, and thick, to set the boys a laughing; nor yet jeered the bald-headed, nor danced the cordax; nor does the old man who speaks the verses beat the person near him with his staff, keeping out of sight wretched ribaldry; nor has she rushed in with torches, nor does she shout iou, iou; but has come relying on herself and her verses. And I, although so excellent a poet, do not give myself airs, nor do I seek to deceive you by twice and thrice bringing forward the same pieces; but I am always clever at introducing new fashions, not at all resembling each other, and all of them clever; who struck Cleon in the belly when at the height of his power, and could not bear to attack him afterward when he was down. But these scribblers, when once Hyperbolus has given them a handle, keep ever trampling on this wretched man and his mother. Eupolis, indeed, first of all craftily introduced his Maricas, having basely, base fellow, spoiled by altering my play of the Knights, having added to it, for the sake of the cordax, a drunken old woman, whom Phrynichus long ago poetized, whom the whale was for devouring. Then again Hermippus made verses on Hyperbolus; and now all others press hard upon Hyperbolus, imitating my simile of the eels.

Whoever, therefore, laughs at these, let him not take pleasure in my attempts; but if you are delighted with me and my inventions, in times to come you will seem to e wise. first invoke, to join our choral band, the mighty Jupiter, ruling on high, the monarch of gods; and the potent master of the trident, the fierce upheaver of earth and briny sea; and our father of great renown, most august Aether, life-supporter of all; and the horse-guider, who fills the plain of the earth with exceeding bright beams, a mighty deity among gods and mortals.

Most clever spectators, come, give us your attention; for having been injured, we blame you to your faces. For though we benefit the state most of all the gods, to us alone of the deities you do not offer sacrifice nor yet pour libations, who watch over you. For if there should be any expedition without prudence, then we either thunder or drizzle small rain. And then, when you were for choosing as your general the Paphlagonian tanner, hateful to the gods, we contracted our brows and were enraged; and thunder burst through the lightning; and the Moon forsook her usual paths; and the Sun immediately drew in his wick to himself, and declared he would not give you light, if Cleon should be your general. Nevertheless you chose him. For they say that ill counsel is in this city; that the gods, however, turn all these your mismanagements to a prosperous issue. And how this also shall be advantageous, we will easily teach you. If you should convict the cormorant Cleon of bribery and embezzlement, and then make fast his neck in the stocks, the affair will turn out for the state to the ancient form again, if you have mismanaged in any way, and to a prosperous issue.

Hear me again, King Phoebus, Delian Apollo, who inhabitest the high-peaked Cynthian rock! And thou, blessed goddess, who inhabitest the all-golden house of Ephesus, in which Lydian damsels greatly reverence thee; and thou, our national goddess, swayer of the aegis, Minerva, guardian of the city! And thou, reveler Bacchus, who, inhabiting the Parnassian rock, sparklest with torches, conspicuous among the Delphic Bacchanals!

When we had got ready to set out hither, the Moon met us, and commanded us first to greet the Athenians and their allies; and then declared that she was angry, for that she had suffered dreadful things, though she benefits you all, not in words, but openly. In the first place, not less than a drachma every month for torches; so that also all, when they went out of an evening, were wont to say, "Boy, don't buy a torch, for the moonlight is beautiful." And she says she confers other benefits on you, but that you do not observe the days at all correctly, but confuse them up and down; so that she ays the gods are constantly threatening her, when they are defrauded of their dinner, and depart home, not having met with the regular feast according to the number of the days. And then, when you ought to be sacrificing, you are inflicting tortures and litigating. And often, while we gods are observing a fast, when we mourn for Memnon or Sarpedon, you are pouring libations and laughing. For which reason Hyperbolus, having obtained the lot this year to be Hieromnemon, was afterward deprived by us gods of his crown; for thus he will know better that he ought to spend the days of his life according to the Moon.

[Enter Socrates]

Soc.
By Respiration, and Chaos, and Air, I have not seen any man so boorish, nor so impracticable, nor so stupid, nor so forgetful; who, while learning some little petty quibbles, forgets them before he has learned them. Nevertheless I will certainly call him out here to the light. Where is Strepsiades? Come forth with your couch.
Strep.
(from within). The bugs do not permit me to bring it forth.
Soc.
Make haste and lay it down; and give me your attention.

[Enter Strepsiades]

Strep.
Very well.
Soc.
Come now; what do you now wish to learn first of those things in none of which you have ever been instructed? Tell me. About measures, or rhythms, or verses?
Strep.
I should prefer to learn about measures; for it is but lately I was cheated out of two choenices by a meal-huckster.
Soc.
I do not ask you this, but which you account the most beautiful measure; the trimetre or the tetrameter?
Strep.
Make a wager then with me, if the semisextarius be not a tetrameter.
Soc.
Go to the devil! How boorish you are and dull of learning. Perhaps you may be able to learn about rhythms.
Strep.
But what good will rhythms do me for a living?
Soc.
In the first place, to be clever at an entertainment, understanding what rhythm is for the war-dance, and what, again, according to the dactyle.
Strep.
According to the dactyle? By Jove, but I know it!
Soc.
Tell me, pray.
Strep.
What else but this finger? Formerly, indeed, when I was yet a boy, this here!
Soc.
You are boorish and stupid.
Strep.

For I do not desire, you wretch, to learn any of these things.
Soc.
What then?
Strep.
That, that, the most unjust cause.
Soc.
But you must learn other things before these; namely, what quadrupeds are properly masculine.
Strep.
I know the males, if I am not mad—krios, tragos, tauros, kuon, alektryon.
Soc.
Do you see what you are doing? You are calling both the female and the male alektryon in the same way.
Strep.
How, pray? Come, tell me.
Soc.
How? The one with you is alektryon, and the other is alektryon also.
Strep.
Yea, by Neptune! How now ought I to call them?
Soc.
The one alektryaina and the other alektor.
Strep.
Alektryaina? Capital, by the Air! So that, in return for this lesson alone, I will fill your kardopos full of barley-meal on all sides.
Soc.
See! See! There again is another blunder! You make kardopos, which is feminine, to be masculine.
Strep.
In what way do I make kardopos masculine?
Soc.
Most assuredly; just as if you were to say Cleonymos.
Strep.

Good sir, Cleonymus had no kneading-trough, but kneaded his bread in a round mortar. How ought I to call it henceforth?
Soc.
How? Call it kardope, as you call Sostrate.
Strep.
Kardope in the feminine?
Soc.
For so you speak it rightly.
Strep.
But that would make it kardope, Kleonyme.
Soc.
You must learn one thing more about names, what are masculine and what of them are feminine.
Strep.
I know what are female.
Soc.
Tell me, pray.
Strep.
Lysilla, Philinna, Clitagora, Demetria.
Soc.
What names are masculine?
Strep.
Thousands; Philoxenus, Melesias, Amynias.
Soc.
But, you wretch! These are not masculine.
Strep.
Are they not males with you?
Soc.
By no means; for how would you call Amynias, if you et him?
Strep.
How would I call? Thus: "Come hither, come hither Amynia!"

Soc.
Do you see ? You call Amynias a woman.
Strep.
Is it not then with justice, who does not serve in the army? But why should I learn these things, that we all know?
Soc.
It is no use, by Jupiter! Having reclined yourself down here—
Strep.
What must I do?
Soc.
Think out some of your own affairs.
Strep.
Not here, pray, I beseech you; but, if I must, suffer me to excogitate these very things on the ground.
Soc.
There is no other way.

[Exit Socrates.]

Strep.
Unfortunate man that I am! What a penalty shall I this day pay to the bugs!
Cho.
Now meditate and examine closely; and roll yourself about in every way, having wrapped yourself up; and quickly, when you fall into a difficulty, spring to another mental contrivance. But let delightful sleep be absent from your eyes.
Strep.
Attatai! Attatai!
Cho.
What ails you? Why are you distressed?
Strep.
Wretched man, I am perishing! The Corinthians, coming out from the bed, are biting me, and devouring my sides, and

drinking up my life-blood, and tearing away my flesh, and digging through my vitals, and will annihilate me.

Cho.
Do not now be very grievously distressed.

Strep.
Why, how, when my money is gone, my complexion gone, my life gone, and my slipper gone? And furthermore in addition to these evils, with singing the night-watches, I am almost gone myself.

[Re-enter Socrates]

Soc.
Ho you! What are you about? Are you not meditating?

Strep.
I? Yea, by Neptune!

Soc.
And what, pray, have you thought?

Strep.
Whether any bit of me will be left by the bugs.

Soc.
You will perish most wretchedly.

Strep.
But, my good friend, I have already perished.

Soc.
You must not give in, but must wrap yourself up; for you have to discover a device for abstracting, and a means of cheating.

[Walks up and down while Strepsiades wraps himself up in the blankets.]

Strep.

Ah me! Would, pray, some one would throw over me\ a swindling contrivance from the sheep-skins.

Soc.
Come now; I will first see this fellow, what he is about. Ho you! Are you asleep?

Strep.
No, by Apollo, I am not!

Soc.
Have you got anything?

Strep.
No; by Jupiter, certainly not!

Soc.
Nothing at all?

Strep.
Nothing, except what I have in my right hand.

Soc.
Will you not quickly cover yourself up and think of something?

Strep.
About what? For do you tell me this, O Socrates!

Soc.
Do you, yourself, first find out and state what you wish.

Strep.
You have heard a thousand times what I wish.
About the interest; so that I may pay no one.

Soc.
Come then, wrap yourself up, and having given your mind play with subtilty, revolve your affairs by little and little, rightly distinguishing and examining.

Strep.
Ah me, unhappy man!

Soc.
Keep quiet; and if you be puzzled in any one of your conceptions, leave it and go; and then set your mind in motion again, and lock it up.

Strep.
(in great glee). O dearest little Socrates!
Soc.
What, old man?
Strep.
I have got a device for cheating them of the interest.
Soc.
Exhibit it.
Strep.
Now tell me this, pray; if I were to purchase a Thessalian witch, and draw down the moon by night, and then shut it up, as if it were a mirror, in a round crest-case, and then carefully keep it-
Soc.
What good, pray, would this do you?
Strep.
What? If the moon were to rise no longer anywhere, I should not pay the interest.
Soc.
Why so, pray?
Strep.
Because the money is lent out by the month.
Soc.
Capital! But I will again propose to you another clever question. If a suit of five talents should be entered against you, tell me how you would obliterate it.
Strep.
How? How? I do not know but I must seek.
Soc.
Do not then always revolve your thoughts about yourself; but slack away your mind into the air, like a cock-chafer tied with a thread by the foot.
Strep.

I have found a very clever method of getting rid of my suit, so that you yourself would acknowledge it.

Soc.

Of what description?

Strep.

Have you ever seen this stone in the chemist's shops, the beautiful and transparent one, from which they kindle fire?

Soc.

Do you mean the burning-glass?

Strep.

I do. Come what would you say, pray, if I were to take this, when the clerk was entering the suit, and were to stand at a distance, in the direction of the sun, thus, and melt out the letters of my suit?

Soc.

Cleverly done, by the Graces!

Strep.

Oh! How I am delighted, that a suit of five talents has been cancelled!

Soc.

Come now, quickly seize upon this.

Strep.

What?

Soc.

How, when engaged in a lawsuit, you could overturn the suit, when you were about to be cast, because you had no witnesses.

Strep.

Most readily and easily.

Soc.

Tell me, pray.

Strep.

Well now, I'll tell you. If, while one suit was still pending, before mine was called on, I were to run away and hang myself.

Soc.
You talk nonsense.
Strep.
By the gods, would I! For no one will bring action against me when I am dead.
Soc.
You talk nonsense. Begone; I can't teach you any longer.
Strep.
Why so? Yea, by the gods, O Socrates!
Soc.
You straightaway forget whatever you learn. For what now was the first thing you were taught? Tell me.
Strep.
Come, let me see: nay, what was the first? What was the fist? Nay, what was the thing in which we knead our flour? Ah me! What was it?
Soc.
Will you not pack off to the devil, you most forgetful and most stupid old man?
Strep.
Ah me, what then, pray will become of me, retched man? For I shall be utterly undone, if I do not earn to ply the tongue. Come, O ye Clouds, give me some good advice.
Cho.
We, old man, advise you, if you have a son grown up, to send him to learn in your stead.
Strep.
Well, I have a fine, handsome son, but he is not willing to learn. What must I do?
Cho.
But do you permit him?
Strep.
Yes, for he is robust in body, and in good health, and is come of the high-plumed dames of Coesyra. I will go for

him, and if he be not willing, I will certainly drive him from my house.

[To Socrates.]

Go in and wait for me a short time.

[Exit]

Cho.
Do you perceive that you are soon to obtain the greatest benefits through us alone of the gods? For this man is ready to do everything that you bid him. But you, while the man is astounded and evidently elated, having perceived it, will quickly fleece him to the best of your power.

[Exit Socrates]

For matters of this sort are somehow accustomed to turn the other way.

[Enter Strepsiades and Phidippides]

Strep.
By Mist, you certainly shall not stay here any longer! But go and gnaw the columns of Megacles.
Phid.
My good sir, what is the matter with you, O father? You are not in your senses, by Olympian Jupiter!
Strep.
See, see, "Olympian Jupiter!" What folly! To think of your believing in Jupiter, as old as you are!
Phid.
Why, pray, did you laugh at this?
Strep.

Reflecting that you are a child, and have antiquated notions. Yet, however, approach, that you may know more; and I will tell you a thing, by learning which you will be a man. But see that you do not teach this to any one.

Phid.

Well, what is it?

Strep.

You swore now by Jupiter.

Phid.

I did.

Strep.

Seest thou, then, how good a thing is learning?
There is no Jupiter, O Phidippides!

Phid.

Who then?

Strep.

Vortex reigns, having expelled Jupiter.

Phid.

Bah! Why do you talk foolishly?

Strep.

Be assured that it is so.

Phid.

Who says this?

Strep.

Socrates the Melian, and Chaerephon, who knows the footmarks of fleas.

Phid.

Have you arrived at such a pitch of frenzy that you believe madmen?

Strep.

Speak words of good omen, and say nothing bad of clever men and wise; of whom, through frugality, none ever shaved or anointed himself, or went to a bath to wash himself; while you squander my property in bathing, as if I were already dead. But go as quickly as possible and learn instead of me.

Phid.
What good could any one learn from them?

Strep.
What, really? Whatever wisdom there is among men.
And you will know yourself, how ignorant and stupid you are. But wait for me here a short time.
[Runs off]

Phid.
Ah me! What shall I do, my father being crazed? Shall I bring him into court and convict him of lunacy, or shall I give information of his madness to the coffin-makers?

[Re-enter Strepsiades with a cock under one arm and a hen under the other]

Strep.
Come, let me see; what do you consider this to be? Tell me.

Phid.
Alectryon.

Strep.
Right. And what this?

Phid.
Alectryon.

Strep.
Both the same? You are very ridiculous. Do not do so, then, for the future; but call this alektryaina, and this one alektor.

Phid.
Alektryaina! Did you learn these clever things by oing in just now to the Titans?

Strep.
And many others too; but whatever I learned on each occasion I used to forget immediately, through length of years.

Phid.

Is it for this reason, pray, that you have also lost your cloak?
Strep.
I have not lost it; but have studied it away.
Phid.
What have you made of your slippers, you foolish man?
Strep.
I have expended them, like Pericles, for needful purposes. Come, move, let us go. And then if you obey your father, go wrong if you like. I also know that I formerly obeyed you, a lisping child of six years old, and bought you a go-cart at the Diasia, with the first obolus I received from the Heliaea.
Phid.
You will assuredly some time at length be grieved at this.
Strep.
It is well done of you that you obeyed. Come hither, come hither O Socrates! Come forth, for I bring to you this son of mine, having persuaded him against his will.

[Enter Socrates]

Soc.
For he is still childish, and not used to the baskets here.
Phid.
You would yourself be used to them if you were hanged.
Strep.
A mischief take you! Do you abuse your teacher?
Soc.
"Were hanged" quoth 'a! How sillily he pronounced it, and with lips wide apart! How can this youth ever learn an acquittal from a trial or a legal summons, or persuasive refutation? And yet Hyperbolus learned this at the cost of a talent.
Strep.
Never mind; teach him. He is clever by nature.

Indeed, from his earliest years, when he was a little fellow only so big, he was wont to form houses and carve ships within-doors, and make little wagons of leather, and make frogs out of pomegranate-rinds, you can't think how cleverly. But see that he learns those two causes; the better, whatever it may be; and the worse, which, by maintaining what is unjust, overturns the better. If not both, at any rate the unjust one by all means.

Soc.
He shall learn it himself from the two causes in person.

[Exit Socrates]

Strep.
I will take my departure. Remember this now, that he is to be able to reply to all just arguments.

[Exit Strepsiades and enter Just Cause and Unjust Cause]

Just Cause.
Come hither! Show yourself to the spectators, although being audacious.

Unjust Cause.
Go whither you please; for I shall far rather do for you, if I speak before a crowd.

Just.
You destroy me? Who are you?

Unj.
A cause.

Just.
Ay, the worse.

Unj.
But I conquer you, who say that you are better than I.

Just.
By doing what clever trick?

Unj.
>By discovering new contrivances.

Just.
>For these innovations flourish by the favour of these silly persons.

Unj.
>No; but wise persons.

Just
>I will destroy you miserably.

Unj.
>Tell me, by doing what?

Just.
>By speaking what is just.

Unj.
>But I will overturn them by contradicting them; for I deny that justice even exists at all.

Just
>Do you deny that it exists?

Unj.
>For come, where is it?

Just
>With the gods.

Unj.
>How, then, if justice exists, has Jupiter not perished, who bound his own father?

Just
>Bah! This profanity now is spreading! Give me a basin.

Unj.
>You are a dotard and absurd.

Just
>You are debauched and shameless.

Unj.
>You have spoken roses of me.

Just

And a dirty lickspittle.

Unj.

You crown me with lilies.

Just

And a parricide.

Unj.

You don't know that you are sprinkling me with gold.

Just

Certainly not so formerly, but with lead.

Unj.

But now this is an ornament to me.

Just

You are very impudent.

Unj.

And you are antiquated.

Just

And through you, no one of our youths is willing to go to school; and you will be found out some time or other by the Athenians, what sort of doctrines you teach the simple-minded.

Unj.

You are shamefully squalid.

Just

And you are prosperous. And yet formerly you were a beggar saying that you were the Mysian Telephus, and gnawing the maxims of Pandeletus out of your little wallet.

Unj.

Oh, the wisdom--

Just

Oh, the madness--

Unj.

Which you have mentioned.

Just

And of your city, which supports you who ruin her youths.

Unj.

You shan't teach this youth, you old dotard.

Just

Yes, if he is to be saved, and not merely to practise loquacity.

Unj.

(to Phidippides) Come hither, and leave him to rave.

Just

You shall howl, if you lay your hand on him.

Cho.

Cease from contention and railing. But show to us, you, what you used to teach the men of former times, and you, the new system of education; in order that, having heard you disputing, he may decide and go to the school of one or the other.

Just.

I am willing to do so.

Unj.

I also am willing.

Cho.

Come now, which of the two shall speak first?

Unj.

I will give him the precedence; and then, from these things which he adduces, I will shoot him dead with new words and thoughts. And at last, if he mutter, he shall be destroyed, being stung in his whole face and his two eyes by my maxims, as if by bees.

Cho.

Now the two, relying on very dexterous arguments and thoughts, and sententious maxims, will show which of them shall appear superior in argument. For now the whole crisis of wisdom is here laid before them; about which my friends have a very great contest. But do you, who adorned our elders with many virtuous manners, utter the voice in which you rejoice, and declare your nature.

Just.
> I will, therefore, describe the ancient system of education, how it was ordered, when I flourished in the advocacy of justice, and temperance was the fashion. In the first place it was incumbent that no one should hear the voice of a boy uttering a syllable; and next, that those from the same quarter of the town should march in good order through the streets to the school of the harp-master, naked, and in a body, even if it were to snow as thick as meal. Then again, their master would teach them, not sitting cross-legged, to learn by rote a song, either "pallada persepolin deinan" or "teleporon ti boama" raising to a higher pitch the harmony which our fathers transmitted to us. But if any of them were to play the buffoon, or to turn any quavers, like these difficult turns the present artists make after the manner of Phrynis, he used to be thrashed, being beaten with many blows, as banishing the Muses. And it behooved the boys, while sitting in the school of the Gymnastic-master, to cover the thigh, so that they might exhibit nothing indecent to those outside; then again, after rising from the ground, to sweep the sand together, and to take care not to leave an impression of the person for their lovers. And no boy used in those days to anoint himself below the navel; so that their bodies wore the appearance of blooming health. Nor used he to go to his lover, having made up his voice in an effeminate tone, prostituting himself with his eyes. Nor used it to be allowed when one was dining to take the head of the radish, or to snatch from their seniors dill or parsley, or to eat fish, or to giggle, or to keep the legs crossed.

Unj.
> Aye, antiquated and dipolia-like and full of grasshoppers, and of Cecydes, and of the Buphonian festival!

Just
> Yet certainly these are those principles by which my system of education nurtured the men who fought at Marathon.

But you teach the men of the present day, so that I am choked, when at the Panathenaia a fellow, lding his shield before his person, neglects Tritogenia, when they ought to dance. Wherefore, O outh, choose with confidence, me, the better cause, and you will learn to hate the Agora, and to refrain from baths, and to be ashamed of what is disgraceful, and to be enraged if any one jeer you, and to rise up from seats before your seniors when they approach, and not to behave ill toward your parents, and to do nothing else that is base, because you are to form in your mind an image of Modesty: and not to dart into the house of a dancing-woman, lest, while gaping after these things, being struck with an apple by a wanton, you should be damaged in your reputation: and not to contradict your father in anything; nor by calling him Iapetus, to reproach him with the ills of age, by which you were reared in your infancy.

Unj.
If you shall believe him in this, O youth, by Bacchus, you will be like the sons of Hippocrates, and they will call you a booby.

Just.
Yet certainly shall you spend your time in the ymnastic schools, sleek and blooming; not chattering in he marketplace rude jests, like the youths of the present day; nor dragged into court for a petty suit, greedy, pettifogging, knavish; but you shall descend to the Academy and run races beneath the sacred olives along with some modest compeer, crowned with white reeds, redolent of yew, and careless ease, of leaf-shedding white poplar, rejoicing in the season of spring, when the plane-tree whispers to the elm. If you do these things which I say, and apply your mind to these, you will ever have a stout chest, a clear complexion, broad shoulders, a little tongue, large hips, little lewdness. But if you practise what the youths of the present day do,

you will have in the first place, a pallid complexion, small shoulders, a narrow chest, a large tongue, little hips, great lewdness, a long psephism; and this deceiver will persuade you to consider everything that is base to be honourable, and what is honourable to be base; and in addition to this, he will fill you with the lewdness of Antimachus.

Cho.

O thou that practisest most renowned high-towering wisdom! How sweetly does a modest grace attend your words! Happy, therefore, were they who lived in those days, in the times of former men! In reply, then, to these, O thou that hast a dainty-seeming Muse, it behooveth thee to say something new; since the man has gained renown. And it appears you have need of powerful arguments against him, if you are to conquer the man and not incur laughter.

Unj.

And yet I was choking in my heart, and was longing to confound all these with contrary maxims. For I have been called among the deep thinkers the "worse cause" on this very account, that I first contrived how to speak against both law and justice; and this art is worth more than ten thousand staters, that one should choose the worse cause, and nevertheless be victorious. But mark how I will confute the system of education on which he relies, who says, in the first place, that he will not permit you to be washed with warm water. And yet, on what principle do you blame the warm baths?

Just.

Because it is most vile, and makes a man cowardly.

Unj.

Stop! For immediately I seize and hold you by the waist without escape. Come, tell me, which of the sons of Jupiter do you deem to have been the bravest in soul, and to have undergone most labours?

Just.

I consider no man superior to Hercules.

Unj.

Where, pray, did you ever see cold Herculean baths?
And yet, who was more valiant than he?

Just.

These are the very things which make the bath full of youths always chattering all day long, but the palaestras empty.

Unj.

You next find fault with their living in the market-place; but I commend it. For if it had been bad, Homer would never have been for representing Nestor as an orator; nor all the other wise men. I will return, then, from thence to the tongue, which this fellow says our youths ought not to exercise, while I maintain they should. And again, he says they ought to be modest: tw very great evils. For tell me to whom you have ever seen any good accrue through modesty and confute me by your words.

Just.

To many. Peleus, at any rate, received his sword n account of it.

Unj.

A sword? Marry, he got a pretty piece of luck, the oor wretch! While Hyperbolus, he of the lamps, got more than many talents by his villainy, but by Jupiter, no
sword!

Just.

And Peleus married Thetis, too, through his modesty.

Unj.

And then she went off and left him; for he was not ustful, nor an agreeable bedfellow to spend the night with. Now a woman delights in being wantonly treated.
But you are an old dotard. For (to Phidippides) consider, O youth, all that attaches to modesty, and of how many plea-

sures you are about to be deprived—of women, of games at cottabus, of dainties, of drinking-bouts, of giggling. And yet, what is life worth to you if you be deprived of these enjoyments? Well, I will pass from thence to the necessities of our nature. You have gone astray, you have fallen in love, you have been guilty of some adultery, and then have been caught. You are undone, for you are unable to speak. But if you associate with me, indulge your inclination, dance, laugh, and think nothing disgraceful. For if you should happen to be detected as an adulterer, you will make this reply to him, " that you have done him no injury": and then refer him to Jupiter, how even he is overcome by love and women . And yet, how could you, who are a mortal, have greater power than a god?

Just.

But what if he should suffer the radish through obeying you, and be depillated with hot ashes? What argument will he be able to state, to prove that he is not a blackguard?

Unj.

And if he be a blackguard, what harm will he suffer?

Just.

Nay, what could he ever suffer still greater than this?

Unj.

What then will you say if you be conquered by me in this?

Just.

I will be silent: what else can I do?

Unj.

Come, now, tell me; from what class do the dvocates come?

Just.

From the blackguards.

Unj.

I believe you. What then? From what class do tragedians come?

Just.

From the blackguards.

Unj.

You say well. But from what class do the public orators come?

Just.

From the blackguards.

Unj.

Then have you perceived that you say nothing to the purpose? And look which class among the audience is the more numerous.

Just.

Well now, I'm looking.

Unj.

What, then, do you see?

Just.

By the gods, the blackguards to be far more numerous. This fellow, at any rate, I know; and him yonder; and this fellow with the long hair.

Unj.

What, then, will you say?

Just.

We are conquered. Ye blackguards, by the gods, receive my cloak, for I desert to you.

[Exeunt the Two Causes, and re-enter Socrates and Strepsiades.]

Soc.

What then? whether do you wish to take and lead away this your son, or shall I teach him to speak?

Strep.

Teach him, and chastise him: and remember that you train him properly; on the one side able for petty suits; but train his other jaw able for the more important causes.

Soc.

Make yourself easy; you shall receive him back a lever sophist.

Strep.
Nay, rather, pale and wretched.

[Exeunt Socrates, Strepsiades, and Phidippides.]

Cho.
Go ye, then: but I think that you will repent of these proceedings. We wish to speak about the judges, what they will gain, if at all they justly assist this Chorus. For in the first place, if you wish to plough up your fields in spring, we will rain for you first; but for the others afterward. And then we will protect the fruits, and the vines, so that neither drought afflict them, nor excessive wet weather. But if any mortal dishonour us who are goddesses, let him consider what evils he will suffer at our hands, obtaining neither wine nor anything else from his farm. For when his olives and vines sprout, they shall be cut down; with such slings will we smite them. And if we see him making brick, we will rain; and we will smash the tiles of his roof with round hailstones. And if he himself, or any one of his kindred or friends, at any time marry, we will rain the whole night; so he will probably wish rather to have been even in Egypt than to have judged badly.

[Enter Strepsiades with a meal-sack on his shoulder.]

Strep.
The fifth, the fourth, the third, after this the second; and then, of all the days I most fear, and dread, and abominate, immediately after this there is the Old and New. For every one to whom I happen to be indebted, swears, and says he will ruin and destroy me, having made his deposits against me; though I only ask what is moderate and just-"My good sir, one part don't take just now; the other part put off I pray; and the other part remit"; they say that thus they will

never get back their money, but abuse me, as I am unjust, and say they will go to law with me. Now therefore let them go to law, for it little concerns me, if Phidippides has learned to speak well. I shall soon know by knocking at the thinking-shop.

[Knocks at the door.]

Boy,
I say! Boy, boy!

[Enter Socrates]

Soc.
Good morning, Strepsiades.

Strep.
The same to you. But first accept this present; for one ought to compliment the teacher with a fee. And tell me about my son, if he has learned that cause, which you just now brought forward.

Soc.
He has learned it.

Strep.
Well done, O Fraud, all-powerful queen!

Soc.
So that you can get clear off from whatever suit you please.

Strep.
Even if witnesses were present when I borrowed\ the money?

Soc.
Yea, much more! Even if a thousand be present.

Strep.
Then I will shout with a very loud shout: Ho! Weep, you petty-usurers, both you and your principals, and your com-

pound interests! For you can no longer do me any harm, because such a son is being reared for me in this house, shining with a double-edged tongue, for my guardian, the preserver of my house, a mischief to my enemies, ending the sadness of the great woes of his father. Him do thou run and summon from within to me.

[Socrates goes into the house.]

O child! O son! Come forth from the house! Hear your ather!

[Re-enter Socrates leading in Phidippides]

Soc.
Lo, here is the man!
Strep.
O my dear, my dear!
Soc.
Take your son and depart.

[Exit Socrates.]

Strep.
Oh, oh, my child! Huzza! Huzza! How I am delighted at the first sight of your complexion! Now, indeed, you are, in the first place, negative and disputatious to look at, and this fashion native to the place plainly appears, the "what do you say?" and the seeming to be injured when, I well know, you are injuring and inflicting a wrong; and in your countenance there is the Attic look. Now, therefore, see that you save me, since you have also ruined me.
Phid.
What, pray, do you fear?
Strep.

The Old and New.
Phid.
Why, is any day old and new?
Strep.
Yes; on which they say that they will make their deposits against me.
Phid.
Then those that have made them will lose them; for it is not possible that two days can be one day.
Strep.
Can not it?
Phid.
Certainly not; unless the same woman can be both old and young at the same time.
Strep.
And yet it is the law.
Phid.
For they do not, I think, rightly understand what the law means.
Strep.
And what does it mean?
Phid.
The ancient Solon was by nature the commons' friend.
Strep.
This surely is nothing whatever to the Old and New.
Phid.
He therefore made the summons for two days, for the Old and New, that the deposits might be made on the first of the month.
Strep.
Why, pray, did he add the old day?
Phid.
In order, my good sir, that the defendants, being present a day before, might compromise the matter of their own

accord; but if not, that they might be worried on the morning of the new moon.

Strep.

Why, then, do the magistrates not receive the deposits on the new moon, but on the Old and New?

Phid.

They seem to me to do what the forestallers do: in order that they may appreciate the deposits as soon as possible, on this account they have the first pick by one day.

Strep.

(turning to the audience) Bravo! Ye wretches, why do you sit senseless, the gain of us wise men, being blocks, ciphers, mere sheep, jars heaped together, wherefore I must sing an encomium upon myself and this my son, on account of our good fortune. "O happy
Strepsiades! How wise you are yourself, and how excellent is the son whom you are rearing!" My friends and fellow-tribesmen will say of me, envying me, when you prove victorious in arguing causes. But first I wish to lead you in and entertain you.

[Exeunt Strepsiades and Phidippides.]

Pasias

(entering with his summons-witness) Then, ought a man to throw away any part of his own property? Never!
But it were better then at once to put away blushes, rather than now to have trouble; since I am now dragging you to be a witness, for the sake of my own money; and further, in addition to this, I shall become an enemy to my fellow-tribesman. But never, while I live, will I disgrace my country, but will summon Strepsiades.

Strep.

(from within) Who's there?

Pas.

For the Old and New.
Strep.
I call you to witness, that he has named it for two days. For what matter do you summon me?
Pas.
For the twelve minae, which you received when you were buying the dapple-gray horse.
Strep.
A horse? Do you not hear? I, whom you all know to hate horsemanship!
Pas.
And, by Jupiter! You swore by the gods too, that you would repay it.
Strep.
Ay, by Jove! For then my Phidippides did not yet know the irrefragable argument.
Pas.
And do you now intend, on this account, to deny the debt?
Strep.
Why, what good should I get else from his instruction?
Pas.
And will you be willing to deny these upon oath of the gods?
Strep.
What gods?
Pas.
Jupiter, Mercury, and Neptune.
Strep.
Yes, by Jupiter! And would pay down, too, a three-obol piece besides to swear.
Pas.
Then may you perish some day for your impudence!
Strep.

This man would be the better for it if he were cleansed by rubbing with salt.

Pas.

Ah me, how you deride me!

Strep.

He will contain six choae.

Pas.

By great Jupiter and the gods, you certainly shall not do this to me with impunity!

Strep.

I like your gods amazingly; and Jupiter, sworn by, is ridiculous to the knowing ones.

Pas.

You will assuredly suffer punishment, some time or other, for this. But answer and dismiss me, whether you are going to repay me my money or not.

Strep.

Keep quiet now, for I will presently answer you distinctly. [Runs into the house.]

Pas.

(to his summons-witness). What do you think he will do?

Witness.

I think he will pay you.

[Re-enter Strepsiades with a kneading-trough]

Strep.

Where is this man who asks me for his money? Tell me what is this?

Pas.

What is this? A kardopos.

Strep.

And do you then ask me for your money, being such an ignorant person? I would not pay, not even an obolus, to any one who called the kardope kardopos.

Pas.

Then won't you pay me?

Strep.
>Not, as far as I know. Will you not then pack off as fast as possible from my door?

Pas.
>I will depart; and be assured of this, that I will make deposit against you, or may I live no longer!

Strep.
>Then you will lose it besides, in addition to your twelve minae. And yet I do not wish you to suffer this, because you named the kardopos floolishly.

[Exeunt Pasias and Witness, and enter Amynias]

Amynias.
>Ah me! Ah me!

Strep.
>Ha! Whoever is this, who is lamenting? Surely it was not one of Carcinus' deities that spoke.

Amyn.
>But why do you wish to know this, who I am?-A miserable man.

Strep.
>Then follow your own path.

Amyn.
>O harsh fortune! O Fates, breaking the wheels of my horses! O Pallas, how you have destroyed me!

Strep.
>What evil, pray, has Tlepolemus ever done you?

Amyn.
>Do not jeer me, my friend; but order your son to pay me the money which he received; especially as I have been unfortunate.

Strep.
>What money is this?

Amyn.
That which he borrowed.
Strep.
Then you were really unlucky, as I think.
Amyn.
By the gods, I fell while driving my horses.
Strep.
Why, pray, do you talk nonsense, as if you had fallen from an ass?
Amyn.
Do I talk nonsense if I wish to recover my money?
Strep.
You can't be in your senses yourself.
Amyn.
Why, pray?
Strep.
You appear to me to have had your brains shaken as it were.
Amyn.
And you appear to me, by Hermes, to be going to be summoned, if you will not pay me the money?
Strep.
Tell me now, whether you think that Jupiter always rains fresh rain on each occasion, or that the sun draws from below the same water back again?
Amyn.
I know not which; nor do I care.
Strep.
How then is it just that you should recover your money, if you know nothing of meteorological matters?
Amyn.
Well, if you are in want, pay me the interest of my money.
Strep.
What sort of animal is this interest?
Amyn.

Most assuredly the money is always becoming more and more every month and every day as the time slips away.

Strep.

You say well. What then? Is it possible that you consider the sea to be greater now than formerly?

Amyn.

No, by Jupiter, but equal; for it is not fitting that it should be greater.

Strep.

And how then, you wretch does this become no way\ greater, though the rivers flow into it, while you seek to increase your money? Will you not take yourself off from my house? Bring me the goad.

[Enter Servant with a goad.]

Amyn.

I call you to witness these things.

Strep.

(beating him). Go! Why do you delay? Won't you march, Mr. Blood-horse?

Amyn.

Is not this an insult, pray?

Strep.

Will you move quickly?
[Pricks him behind with the goad.]
I'll lay on you, goading you behind, you outrigger? Do you fly?

[Amynias runs off.]

I thought I should stir you, together with your wheels and your two-horse chariots.

[Exit Strepsiades.]

Cho.
What a thing it is to love evil courses! For this old man, having loved them, wishes to withhold the money that he borrowed. And he will certainly meet with something today, which will perhaps cause this sophist to suddenly receive some misfortune, in return for the knaveries he has begun. For I think that he will presently find what has been long boiling up, that his son is skilful to speak opinions opposed to justice, so as to overcome all with whomsoever he holds converse, even if he advance most villainous doctrines; and perhaps, perhaps his father will wish that he were even speechless.

Strep.
(running out of the house pursued by his son) Hollo! Hollo! O neighbours, and kinsfolk, and fellow-tribesmen, defend me, by all means, who am being beaten! Ah me, unhappy man, for my head and jaw! Wretch!
Do you beat your father?

Phid.
Yes, father.

Strep.
You see him owning that he beats me.

Phid.
Certainly.

Strep.
O wretch, and parricide, and house-breaker!

Phid.
Say the same things of me again, and more. Do you\ know that I take pleasure in being much abused?

Strep.
You blackguard!

Phid.
Sprinkle me with roses in abundance.

Strep.
Do you beat your father?
Phid.
And will prove too, by Jupiter! that I beat you with justice.
Strep.
O thou most rascally! Why, how can it be just to beat a father?
Phid.
I will demonstrate it, and will overcome you in argument.
Strep.
Will you overcome me in this?
Phid.
Yea, by much and easily. But choose which of the wo Causes you wish to speak.
Strep.
Of what two Causes?
Phid.
The better, or the worse?
Strep.
Marry, I did get you taught to speak against justice, by Jupiter, my friend, if you are going to persuade me of this, that it is just and honourable for a father to be beaten by his sons!
Phid.
I think I shall certainly persuade you; so that, when you have heard, not even you yourself will say anything against it.
Strep.
Well, now, I am willing to hear what you have to say.
Cho.
It is your business, old man, to consider in what way you shall conquer the man; for if he were not relying upon something, he would not be so licentious. But he is emboldened by something; the boldness of the man is evident.

Now you ought to tell to the Chorus from what the contention first arose. And this you must do by all means.

Strep.

Well, now, I will tell you from what we first began to rail at one another. After we had feasted, as you know, I first bade him take a lyre, and sing a song of Simonides, "The Shearing of the Ram." But he immediately said it was old-fashioned to play on the lyre and sing while drinking, like a woman grinding parched barley.

Phid.

For ought you not then immediately to be beaten and trampled on, bidding me sing, just as if you were entertaining cicadae?

Strep.

He expressed, however, such opinions then too within, as he does now; and he asserted that Simonides was a bad poet. I bore it at first, with difficulty indeed, yet nevertheless I bore it. And then I bade him at least take a myrtle-wreath and recite to me some portion of Aeschylus; and then he immediately said, "Shall I consider Aeschylus the first among the poets, full of empty sound, unpolished, bombastic, using rugged words?" And hereupon you can't think how my heart panted. But, nevertheless, I restrained my passion, and said, "At least recite some passage of the more modern poets, of whatever kind these clever things be." And he immediately sang a passage of Euripides, how a brother, O averter of ill! Debauched his uterine sister. And I bore it no longer, but immediately assailed him with many abusive reproaches. And then, after that, as was natural, we hurled word upon word. Then he springs upon me; and then he was wounding me, and beating me, and throttling me.

Phid.

Were you not therefore justly beaten, who do not praise Euripides, the wisest of poets?

Strep.

He the wisest! Oh, what shall I call you? But I shall be beaten again.

Phid.

Yes, by Jupiter, with justice?

Strep.

Why, how with justice? Who, O shameless fellow, reared you, understanding all your wishes, when you lisped what you meant? If you said bryn, I, understanding it, used to give you to drink. And when you asked for mamman, I used to come to you with bread. And you used no sooner to say caccan, than I used to take and carry you out of doors, and hold you before me. But you now, throttling me who was bawling and crying out because I wanted to ease myself, had not the heart to carry me forth out of doors, you wretch; but I did it there while I was being throttled. Cho. I fancy the hearts of the youths are panting to hear what he will say. For if, after having done such things, he shall persuade him by speaking, I would not take the hide of the old folks, even at the price of a chick-pea. It is thy business, thou author and upheaver of new words, to seek some means of persuasion, so that you shall seem to speak justly.

Phid.

How pleasant it is to be acquainted with new and clever things, and to be able to despise the established laws! For I, when I applied my mind to horsemanship alone, used not to be able to utter three words before I made a mistake; but now, since he himself has made me cease from these pursuits, and I am acquainted with subtle thoughts, and arguments, and speculations, I think I shall demonstrate that it is just to chastise one's father.

Strep.

Ride, then, by Jupiter! Since it is better for me to keep a team of four horses than to be killed with a beating.

Phid.

I will pass over to that part of my discourse where you interrupted me; and first I will ask you this: Did you beat me when I was a boy?

Strep.

I did, through good-will and concern for you.

Phid.

Pray tell me, is it not just that I also should be well inclined toward you in the same way, and beat you, since this is to be well inclined-to give a beating? For why ought your body to be exempt from blows and mine not? And yet I too was born free. The boys weep, and do you not think it is right that a father should weep? You will say that it is ordained by law that this should be the lot of boys. But I would reply, that old men are boys twice over, and that it is the more reasonable that the old should weep than the young, inasmuch as it is less just that they should err.

Strep.

It is nowhere ordained by law that a father should suffer this.

Phid.

Was it not then a man like you and me, who first proposed this law, and by speaking persuaded the ancients? Why then is it less lawful for me also in turn to propose henceforth a new law for the sons, that they should beat their fathers in turn? But as many blows as we received before the law was made, we remit: and we concede to them our having been thrashed without return. Observe the cocks and these other animals, how they punish their fathers; and yet, in what do they differ from us, except that they do not write decrees?

Strep.

Why then, since you imitate the cocks in all things, do you not both eat dung and sleep on a perch?

Phid.

It is not the same thing, my friend; nor would it appear so to Socrates.

Strep.

Therefore do not beat me; otherwise you will one day blame yourself.

Phid.

Why, how?

Strep.

Since I am justly entitled to chastise you; and you to chastise your son, if you should have one.

Phid.

But if I should not have one, I shall have wept for nothing, and you will die laughing at me.

Strep.

To me, indeed, O comrades, he seems to speak justly; and I think we ought to concede to them what is itting. For it is proper that we should weep, if we do not act justly.

Phid.

Consider still another maxim.

Strep.

No; for I shall perish if I do.

Phid.

And yet perhaps you will not be vexed at suffering what you now suffer.

Strep.

How, pray? For inform me what good you will do me by this.

Phid.

I will beat my mother, just as I have you.

Strep.

What do you say? What do you say? This other, again, is a greater wickedness.

Phid.

But what if, having the worst Cause, I shall conquer you in arguing, proving that it is right to beat one's mother?

Strep.
Most assuredly, if you do this, nothing will hinder you from casting yourself and your Worse Cause into the pit along with Socrates. These evils have I suffered through you, O Clouds! Having intrusted all my affairs to you.

Cho.
Nay, rather, you are yourself the cause of these things, having turned yourself to wicked courses.

Strep.
Why, pray, did you not tell me this, then, but excited with hopes a rustic and aged man?

Cho.
We always do this to him whom we perceive to be a lover of wicked courses, until we precipitate him into misfortune, so that he may learn to fear the gods.

Strep.
Ah me ! it is severe, O Clouds! But it is just; for I ought not to have withheld the money which I borrowed. Now, therefore, come with me, my dearest son, hat you may destroy the blackguard Chaerephon and Socrates, who deceived you and me.

Phid.
I will not injure my teachers.

Strep.
Yes, yes, reverence Paternal Jove.

Phid.
"Paternal Jove" quoth'a! How antiquated you are! Why, is there any Jove?

Strep.
There is.

Phid.
There is not, no; for Vortex reigns having expelled Jupiter.

Strep.

He has not expelled him; but I fancied this, on account of this Vortex here. Ah me, unhappy man! When I even took you who are of earthenware for a god.

Phid.
Here rave and babble to yourself.

[Exit Phidippides]

Strep.
Ah me, what madness! How mad, then, I was when I jected the gods on account of Socrates! But O dear Hermes, by no means be wroth with me, nor destroy me; but pardon me, since I have gone crazy through prating. And become my adviser, whether I shall bring an action and prosecute them, or whatever you think. You advise me rightly, not permitting me to get up a lawsuit, but as soon as possible to set fire to the house of the prating fellows. Come hither, come hither, Xanthias! Come forth with a ladder and with a mattock and then mount upon the thinking-shop and dig down the roof, if you love your master, until you tumble the house upon them.

[Xanthias mounts upon the roof]

But let some one bring me a lighted torch and I'll make some of them this day suffer punishment, even if they be ever so much impostors.

1st Dis.
(from within) Hollo! Hollo!

Strep.
t is your business, O torch, to send forth abundant flame.

[Mounts upon the roof]

1st Dis.
What are you doing, fellow?

Strep.
What am I doing? Why, what else, than chopping logic with the beams of your house?

[Sets the house on fire]

2nd Dis.
(from within) You will destroy us! You will destroy us!

Strep.
For I also wish this very thing; unless my mattock deceive my hopes, or I should somehow fall first and break my neck.

Soc.
(from within). Hollo you! What are you doing, pray, you fellow on the roof?

Strep.
I am walking on air, and speculating about the sun.

Soc.
Ah me, unhappy! I shall be suffocated, wretched an!

Chaer.
And I, miserable man, shall be burnt to death!

Strep.
For what has come into your heads that you acted insolently toward the gods, and pried into the seat of the moon? Chase, pelt, smite them, for many reasons, but especially because you know that they offended against the gods!

[The thinking shop is burned down]

Cho.
Lead the way out; for we have sufficiently acted as chorus for today.

[Exeunt omnes]

www.ingramcontent.com/pod-product-compliance
Lightning Source LLC
Chambersburg PA
CBHW051552010526
44118CB00022B/2676